T0067042

Presented to:

From:

ZONDERKIDZ

The Beginner's Bible® 100 Bedtime Devotions

Requests for information should be addressed to:
Zonderkidz, *3900 Sparks Drive SE, Grand Rapids, Michigan 49546*

Hardcover ISBN 978-0-310-14256-0
Ebook ISBN 978-0-310-14259-1
Audio Download ISBN 978-0-310-15860-8

Library of Congress Cataloging-in-Publication Data

Names: Bowman, Crystal, author.
Title: The beginner's Bible 100 bedtime devotions : thoughts and prayers to end your day / Crystal Bowman.
Description: Grand Rapids : Zonderkidz, 2023. | Audience: Ages 4-8 | Summary: "Snuggle up for some special time with God and your little one! The Beginner's Bible Bedtime Devotions contains 100 devotions that are fun and accessible for young children, so you can end the day by reassuring your child of God's amazing love for them. The Beginner's Bible 100 Bedtime Devotions is a cozy, faith-filled addition to any bedtime routine. With devotions organized by theme-including gratitude, courage, friendship, peace, and more-it's easy to find the perfect message for anything that's on a child's heart or mind"-- Provided by publisher.
Identifiers: LCCN 2022034842 (print) | LCCN 2022034843 (ebook) | ISBN 9780310142560 (hardcover) | ISBN 9780310142591 (ebook)
Subjects: LCSH: Bible--Devotional literature--Juvenile literature. | Children--Prayers and devotions. | Christian children--Prayers and devotions.
Classification: LCC BV4870 .B635 2023 (print) | LCC BV4870 (ebook) | DDC 242/.82--dc23/eng/20230103
LC record available at https://lccn.loc.gov/2022034842
LC ebook record available at https://lccn.loc.gov/2022034843

Illustrations: Denis Alonso
Content Contributor: Crystal Bowman
Design: Diane Mielke

Printed in India

---

23 24 25 26 27 28/REP/10 9 8 7 6 5 4 3 2 1

The Beginner's Bible

100 Bedtime Devotions

Thoughts and Prayers to End Your Day

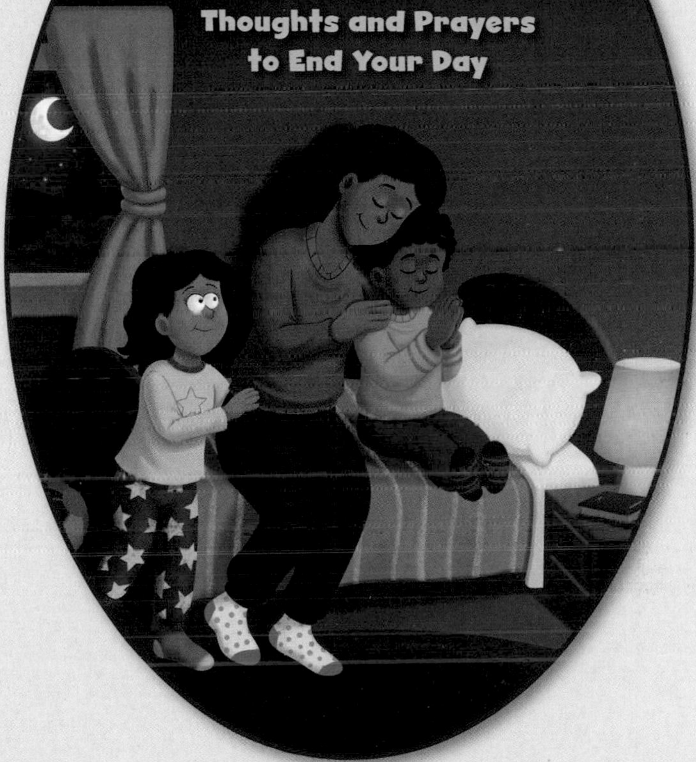

ZONDERkidz

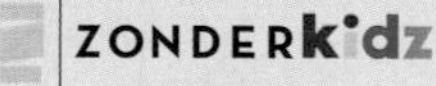

Table of Contents

FAMILY AND FRIENDS

Night 1 The First Family 10
Night 2 God's Promise to Abraham 11
Night 3 A Wife for Isaac 12
Night 4 Ruth and Naomi 13
Night 5 Two Best Friends 14
Night 6 Elijah and Elisha 15
Night 7 Twelve Special Friends 16
Night 8 Four Good Friends 17
Night 9 Two Sad Sisters 18
Night 10 God's Big Family 19

HAVE COURAGE

Night 11 God Speaks to Moses 22
Night 12 A Scary Night 23
Night 13 Two Brave Spies 24
Night 14 A Mighty Warrior 25
Night 15 A Boy and a Giant 26
Night 16 Brave Queen Esther 27
Night 17 Daniel's Night with the Lions 28
Night 18 Don't Worry 29
Night 19 Who Is That? 30
Night 20 The Prison Guard 31

BE WISE

Night 21 Abraham's Good Idea 34
Night 22 Joseph Helps Pharaoh 35
Night 23 Judge Deborah 36
Night 24 God Speaks to Samuel 37
Night 25 Wise King Solomon 38
Night 26 Naaman Finally Listens 39
Night 27 King Josiah 40
Night 28 The Wise Men 41
Night 29 The Better Choice 42
Night 30 Wisdom from the Holy Spirit 43

PRAISE AND THANKSGIVING

Night 31 Noah Honors God 46
Night 32 Free at Last 47
Night 33 Hannah's Joy 48
Night 34 Songs of Praise 49
Night 35 A New Place to Worship 50
Night 36 Happy Shepherds 51
Night 37 One Thankful Man 52
Night 38 Mary's Special Gift 53
Night 39 Praise the King 54
Night 40 Jumping for Joy 55

BULLYING, JEALOUSY, AND MEANNESS

Night 41 Jacob Is Jealous 58
Night 42 Joseph's Mean Brothers 59
Night 43 A Stubborn King 60
Night 44 The Wrong Friends 61
Night 45 A Jealous King 62
Night 46 Nebuchadnezzar's Bad Idea 63
Night 47 Mean King Herod 64
Night 48 Bully Tax Collectors 65
Night 49 Enemies of Jesus 66
Night 50 Jesus Changes a Mean Man's Heart 67

FORGIVING HEARTS

Night 51 Adam and Eve Disobey 70
Night 52 Esau Forgives Jacob 71
Night 53 God Meant It for Good 72
Night 54 God Forgives Nineveh's People 73
Night 55 John the Baptist 74
Night 56 The Lord's Prayer 75
Night 57 A Forgiving Father 76
Night 58 Zacchaeus Meets Jesus 77
Night 59 A Special Supper 78
Night 60 Jesus Forgives 79

SERVE WITH KINDNESS

Night 61 Abraham's Visitors 82
Night 62 Rahab Protects the Spies 83
Night 63 Ruth and Boaz 84
Night 64 Elijah Helps a Poor Widow 85
Night 65 Lots of Jars 86
Night 66 Elisha's Kind Friends 87
Night 67 Six Water Jugs 88
Night 68 A Boy Shares His Lunch 89
Night 69 Jesus Heals a Blind Man 90
Night 70 Jesus Serves His Disciples 91

PEACE, HOPE, AND PATIENCE

Night 71 Jacob Has a Dream 94
Night 72 God Feeds the Israelites 95
Night 73 Elijah and the Birds 96
Night 74 Mary's Special Message 97
Night 75 Jesus Is Born 98
Night 76 Peace on Earth 99
Night 77 Simeon Sees Jesus 100
Night 78 A Commander's Faith 101
Night 79 Jesus Calms a Stormy Sea 102
Night 80 Jesus Is Coming Back 103

LOVING GOD AND LOVING OTHERS

Night 81 Noah Loved God 106
Night 82 The Ten Commandments 107
Night 83 David's Heart for God 108
Night 84 David's Sheep 109
Night 85 The One True God 110
Night 86 Anna at the Temple 111
Night 87 The Good Neighbor 112
Night 88 The Widow's Coins 113
Night 89 Do You Love Me? 114
Night 90 Paul Shares the Good News 115

GOD'S PURPOSE FOR US

Night 91 God's Big World 118
Night 92 The Tall Tower 119
Night 93 God's Plans for Baby Moses 120
Night 94 A Cloud over the Tent 121
Night 95 God's Purpose for John 122
Night 96 The Good Fish 123
Night 97 The Lost Sheep 124
Night 98 Jesus and the Children 125
Night 99 Jesus's Message to His Disciples 126
Night 100 New Believers Meet Together 127

Note to Parents

Children love reading and sharing—especially at bedtime. Establishing a routine at the end of the day helps a child relax and unwind before going to sleep. This is also the perfect time to read kid-friendly Bible stories or devotions with your children to help them grow in their faith and knowledge of God.

The devotions in this book are based on Bible stories from *The Beginner's Bible*. They are arranged according to topic so you can read them in order or skip around to find the one that addresses a concern that's on your child's mind.

Topics are:

Family and Friends

Have Courage

Be Wise

Praise and Thanksgiving

Bullying, Jealousy, and Meanness

Forgiving Hearts

Serve with Kindness

Peace, Hope, and Patience

Loving God and Loving Others

God's Purpose for Us

Each devotion includes a Bible verse, a brief retelling of a Bible story, and a personal message to help young listeners apply the truth of God's Word to their everyday lives. The devotions conclude with a short nighttime prayer that encourages children to talk to God about anything that's on their mind.

It's our prayer that these devotions will inspire meaningful conversations between you and your children as they settle in for a good night's sleep. As you read, talk, and pray together, may you be blessed with the wisdom, hope, and peace that come from spending time with God.

Family and Friends

The L*ORD* *God said, "It is not good for the man to be alone. I will make a helper who is just right for him."*

Genesis 2:18

Night 1

The First Family

When God created the world, he created a man named Adam and placed him in a beautiful garden called Eden. God knew Adam needed a friend, so he created a woman named Eve. Adam and Eve were the first husband and wife to live on earth. When they had children, they became the very first family.

From the very beginning, families were important to God. He wants us to be surrounded by people who love us.

My Bedtime Prayer

Thank you, God, tonight and every night, for making families.

The LORD took Abram outside and said, "Look up at the sky. Count the stars, if you can." Then he said to him, "That's how many children will be born into your family."

Genesis 15:5

Night 2

God's Promise to Abraham

Abraham and Sarah were sad because they didn't have any children. But God promised, "I will bless you with many children. Your great-great grandchildren will be like the stars—too many to count!" Even though Abraham and Sarah were old, God gave them a baby boy, and many years later, God's promise came true. Abraham's family had too many people to count!

God promises us wonderful things. A loving family is a beautiful blessing.

My Bedtime Prayer

Thank you, God, for always keeping your promises.

"Promise me that you will go to my country and to my own relatives. Get a wife for my son Isaac from there."

Genesis 24:4

Night 3

A Wife for Isaac

Abraham sent his servant to their hometown to find a girl for his son Isaac to marry. The servant knew this was an important job, so he asked God to help him. God answered his prayer and sent Rebekah to meet him at a well. Because of her kindness, the servant knew she was the right one.

God cares about who joins our family, and he cares about who we choose as friends. We can ask him to bring the right people into our lives.

My Bedtime Prayer

Lord, thank you for the friends and family you bring into my life.

But Ruth replied, "Don't try to make me leave you and go back. Where you go I'll go. Where you stay I'll stay. Your people will be my people. Your God will be my God."

Ruth 1:16

Night 4

Ruth and Naomi

Naomi was sad because her husband and two sons had died. Her daughter-in-law Ruth loved Naomi and wanted to take care of her. When Naomi planned to go back to her home in Israel, she told Ruth to stay in her own land. But Ruth said, "I will go where you go." God blessed Ruth for being a good daughter-in-law to Naomi.

When we are kind to the people in our family and show them love, God will bless us too.

My Bedtime Prayer

Lord, help me to care about and be kind to the people in my family, tomorrow and always.

Jonathan had David promise his friendship again because he loved him. In fact, Jonathan loved David just as he loved himself.

1 Samuel 20:17

Night 5

Two Best Friends

Jonathan was the son of King Saul, but God chose David to be the next king instead of Jonathan. Rather than being jealous of David, Jonathan was David's best friend. Jonathan even protected David when King Saul wanted to hurt him. David and Jonathan promised to be best friends forever, even if they were far apart.

God wants us to care about our friends and treat them the way we want to be treated.

My Bedtime Prayer

God, help me be a good friend to everyone I meet.

They said, "The spirit of Elijah has been given to Elisha."

2 Kings 2:15

Night 6

Elijah and Elisha

Elijah was a prophet who told people about God's love. God gave Elijah a friend and helper named Elisha who learned many things from Elijah. When Elijah was old, Elisha said, "Please give me a double share of the spirit God has given to you." When Elijah went to heaven, God gave Elisha what he asked for.

When our friends see how much we love God, they may want to love God too!

My Bedtime Prayer

Fill me with your Spirit, Lord,
so I can love you more each day.

When morning came, he called for his disciples to come to him. He chose 12 of them and made them apostles.

Luke 6:13

Night 7

Twelve Special Friends

Jesus had many friends when he lived on earth. They would listen to him as he talked about God's love. Jesus had twelve special friends called apostles or disciples. He asked each one to leave their homes and follow him so they could be his helpers. Jesus wants to be your friend too. You don't need to leave your home—you can follow Jesus by loving him and sharing his love with your friends and family.

My Bedtime Prayer

Jesus, I want to be your friend.
Help me follow you every day.

But they could not get him close to Jesus because of the crowd. So they made a hole by digging through the roof above Jesus. Then they lowered the man through it on a mat.

Mark 2:4

Night 8

Four Good Friends

Four men had a friend who couldn't walk. They brought him to a house where Jesus was teaching, but it was crowded inside. They carried their friend to the roof and lowered him down in front of Jesus. "Your sins are forgiven," Jesus said. "Pick up your mat and walk." The man stood up and walked out the door, praising God.

Jesus is happy when we care about our friends and try to help them. When we pray for our friends, we can ask God to bless them.

My Bedtime Prayer

Jesus, help me share your love with my friends tomorrow.

When Jesus heard this, he said, "This sickness will not end in death. No, it is for God's glory. God's Son will receive glory because of it."

John 11:4

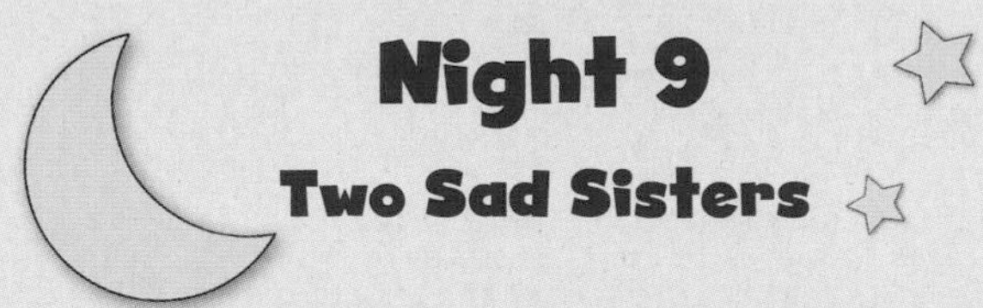

Night 9

Two Sad Sisters

Mary and Martha were friends of Jesus. When their brother, Lazarus, became sick, Martha sent a message for Jesus to come quickly. Lazarus died before Jesus arrived. The sisters cried when they saw Jesus, and he cried too. Jesus prayed to God out loud so everyone would know God's power was in him. Then he said, "Lazarus, come out!" And Lazarus walked out of the tomb!

Jesus showed everyone how much he loved and cared about his friends. He wants us to love our friends too.

My Bedtime Prayer

You love people so much, Jesus! Help me love others every day, the same way you do.

Every day they met together in the temple courtyard. They ate meals together in their homes. Their hearts were glad and sincere.

Acts 2:46

Night 10

God's Big Family

After Jesus went to heaven, his followers told everyone about Jesus. The people who believed in Jesus were called Christians. They would meet in homes to sing and pray and talk about God. They would even eat meals together. They were like one big happy family.

Did you know that you can become part of God's family? If you believe in Jesus as your Savior, then you are part of God's big family.

My Bedtime Prayer

Thank you, God, for reminding me tonight that I can be part of your family by believing in Jesus.

Have Courage

God said, "I will be with you. I will give you a sign. It will prove that I have sent you.

Exodus 3:12

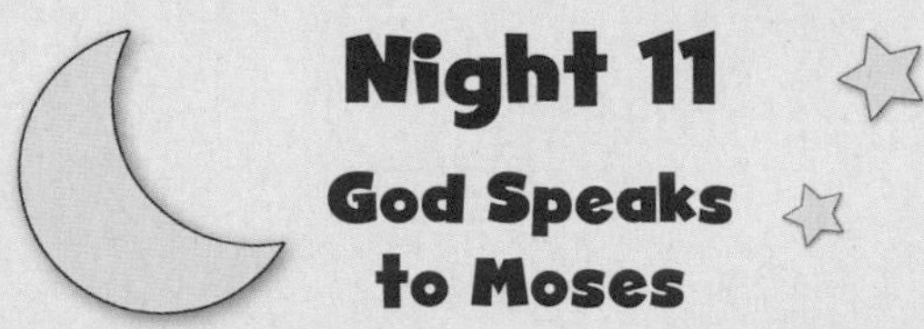

Night 11

God Speaks to Moses

Moses grew up in Egypt, but then he became a shepherd in Midian. One day he saw a bush that was on fire. God spoke to Moses from the bush and said, "I'm sending you to Egypt to rescue my people from Pharaoh." Moses was afraid and didn't want to go. But God promised to be with him and help him.

If you are afraid to do something, remember that God is with you. He will help you too.

My Bedtime Prayer

Thank you, Lord, that you help me when I am afraid.

Moses answered the people. He said, "Don't be afraid. Stand firm. You will see how the LORD will save you today."

Exodus 14:13

Night 12

A Scary Night

The Israelites escaped from Egypt during the night. When they made it to the Red Sea, they thought they were trapped and cried out to Moses. Pharaoh's army was chasing them and would soon catch up with them. God told Moses, "Raise your staff over the sea!" Suddenly the sea parted, and the people walked on a path to the other side.

When things seem impossible, call out to God and see what he can do.

My Bedtime Prayer

Lord, you can do impossible things!
I trust in you.

The LORD said to Moses, "Send some men to check out the land of Canaan. I am giving it to the Israelites. Send one leader from each of Israel's tribes."

Numbers 13:1–2

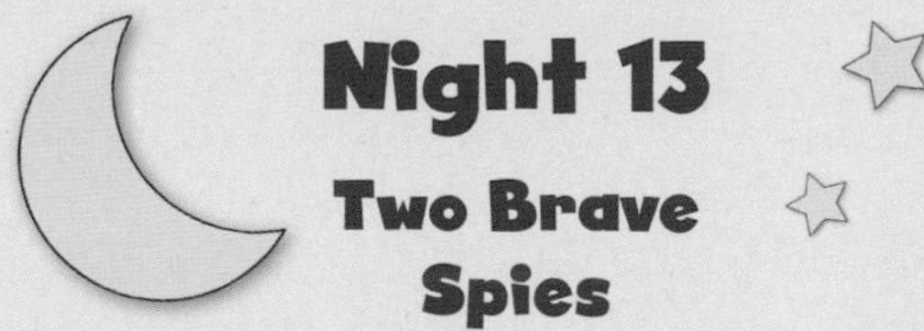

Night 13

Two Brave Spies

When the Israelites were getting closer to the Promised Land, Moses sent 12 spies to see what it was like. Ten spies came back afraid and said, "The people are big and strong, and the city has tall walls around it." But Joshua and Caleb were brave and said, "The land is beautiful and filled with delicious food. God will give us the land he promised."

When we believe God's promises like Joshua and Caleb, we don't have to be afraid.

My Bedtime Prayer

Help me remember your promises, Lord, especially when I feel scared.

"Pardon me, sir," Gideon replied, "but how can I possibly save Israel? My family group is the weakest in the tribe of Manasseh. And I'm the least important member of my family."

Judges 6:15

Night 14

A Mighty Warrior

God sent an angel to a man named Gideon. "The Lord is with you, mighty warrior," the angel said. "God wants you to save his people from the Midianites." Gideon didn't feel like a warrior. His family was not important. But God told Gideon what to do and he helped Gideon rescue the Israelites.

You don't need to be important for God to use you. If you listen to God and trust him, he can help you do amazing things.

My Bedtime Prayer

Lord, I am glad you can use me to do important things today, tomorrow, and every day.

"The LORD *saved me from the paw of the lion. He saved me from the paw of the bear. And he'll save me from the powerful hand of this Philistine too."*

1 Samuel 17:37

Night 15

A Boy and a Giant

Goliath was a big, mean giant. No one dared to fight him, except for David, a young shepherd boy. David was braver than all the soldiers of Israel because he knew God would help him. David picked up five stones and put one in his sling. He whirled it around and the stone hit Goliath's forehead. Bam! The giant tumbled to the ground!

When you need to be brave, remember that God is bigger and stronger than any problems you have.

My Bedtime Prayer

Tomorrow I will be brave and strong because you are with me, Lord.

"Who knows? It's possible that you became queen for a time just like this."

Esther 4:14

Night 16

Brave Queen Esther

Queen Esther was afraid because her husband, the king, made a law to get rid of the Jewish people. The king didn't know Esther was Jewish. But instead of hiding it from him, she told him the truth. Esther put her own life in danger to try and save her people. She thought the king would be angry with her, but he wasn't. He changed the law. God used Esther to save the Jewish people.

Sometimes it can be scary to talk about something that's bothering you. But it's always best to tell the truth. Ask God to help you know the right words to say.

My Bedtime Prayer

Lord, please give me courage to speak when I need to.

"My God sent his angel. And his angel shut the mouths of the lions. They haven't hurt me at all. That's because I haven't done anything wrong in God's sight."

Daniel 6:22

Night 17

Daniel's Night with the Lions

Daniel was the king's best helper. The other helpers were jealous and didn't like him. The men told King Darius to make a law that everyone must pray only to him. Daniel didn't obey that law—he obeyed God instead. He kept praying to God and got thrown in a lions' den for a whole night. Daniel wasn't afraid, and God protected him.

When someone tells you to do something you know is wrong, remember that obeying God is always right.

My Bedtime Prayer

Lord, give me courage to obey you every day, even when it's hard.

"So don't worry. Don't say, 'What will we eat?' Or, 'What will we drink?' Or, 'What will we wear?'"

Matthew 6:31

Night 18

Don't Worry

One day, Jesus stood on a hill so everyone could see him and hear him teach. "Don't worry about anything," he said. "God gives food to the birds, and he dresses the flowers in beautiful colors. You are more important than they are, so God will take care of you too."

Jesus's words are true for us today. When you feel scared or worried, remember that God takes care of the flowers and birds, so you can trust him to take care of you.

My Bedtime Prayer

Thank you, Lord, that I do not need to worry because you take good care of me.

[The disciples] saw him walking on the lake. They thought he was a ghost, so they cried out. They all saw him and were terrified. Right away Jesus said to them, "Be brave! It is I. Don't be afraid."

Mark 6:49–50

Night 19

Who Is That?

One night the disciples were in their boat while Jesus stayed on shore. Suddenly, the weather got stormy, and Jesus knew his disciples needed help. As Jesus walked toward them on top of the water, they cried out in fear because they thought he was a ghost. But as soon as Jesus got into their boat, the storm stopped.

When scary things happen, remember that Jesus is always with you, no matter where you are. He can calm any storm.

My Bedtime Prayer

Thank you, Jesus, that you are with me tonight and always.

"Don't harm yourself!" Paul shouted. "We are all here!"
The jailer called out for some lights. He rushed in, shaking with fear.
He fell down in front of Paul and Silas.

Acts 16:28–29

Night 20

The Prison Guard

Paul and Silas were in prison for telling people about Jesus. One night, an earthquake shook the doors open, and the chains fell off the prisoners. The guard was terrified and thought the prisoners had escaped, but they hadn't. He asked Paul and Silas what to do. "Believe in Jesus and you will be saved!" they said. The prison guard believed and was baptized.

Being afraid can bring us closer to God. When we believe in Jesus, he takes away our fear.

My Bedtime Prayer

Jesus, thank you for being my Savior.
Help me to keep believing in you.

Be Wise

"Isn't the whole land in front of you? Let's separate. If you go to the left, I'll go to the right. If you go to the right, I'll go to the left."

Genesis 13:9

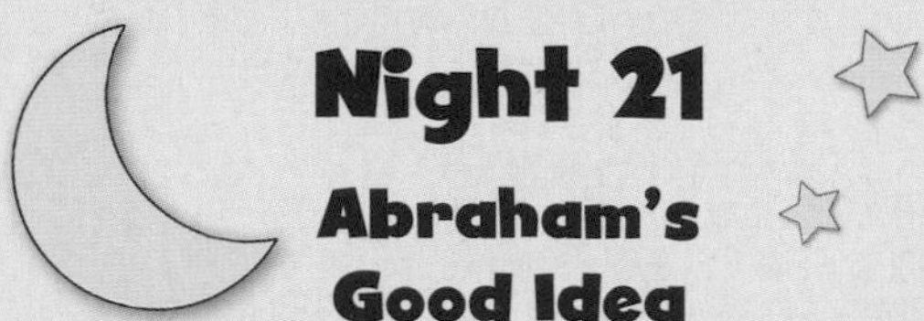

Night 21

Abraham's Good Idea

God told Abraham to move to a new land. His wife Sarah, nephew Lot, and many helpers went along. Soon it was too crowded, and the helpers began to argue. Abraham was wise. He knew there was enough land for everyone. He told Lot, "Choose the land you want, and I'll go the other way."

When your friends disagree, ask God to give you wisdom to work things out.

My Bedtime Prayer

Lord, when problems come, help me to act wisely and know what to do.

Then Pharaoh said to Joseph, "God has made all this known to you. No one is as wise and understanding as you are."

Genesis 41:39

Night 22

Joseph Helps Pharaoh

Joseph was living in Egypt when Pharaoh had some unusual dreams. God helped Joseph understand the meaning of Pharaoh's dreams, so Pharaoh put him in charge of preparing the land of Egypt for a great famine. "You are very wise," said Pharaoh. But Joseph said, "God has shown you what he is going to do." Joseph knew his wisdom came from God.

When you are not sure about something, ask God to help you understand what he wants you to do.

My Bedtime Prayer

Lord, please give me your wisdom and insight for all my days.

Under the Palm Tree of Deborah she served the people as their judge. . . . They came to have her decide cases for them. She settled matters between them.

Judges 4:5

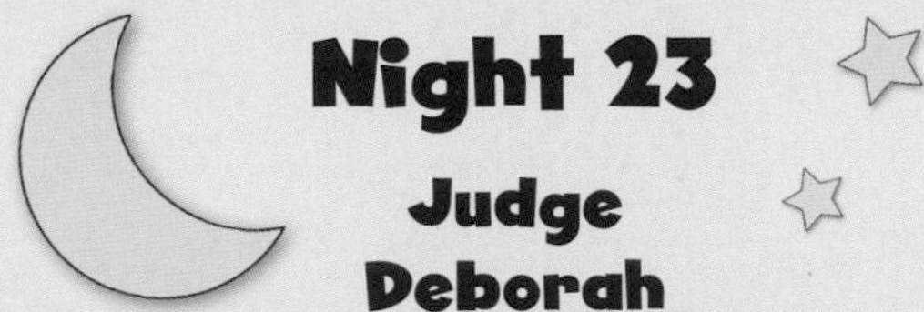

Night 23

Judge Deborah

God sent people called judges to help lead the Israelites when they lived in the Promised Land. Deborah was a wise judge who helped the Israelites follow God. When God wanted his people to fight an evil king, he gave Deborah a plan to help the Israelites win the battle. Then Deborah praised God for their victory.

The best way to be a wise leader is by helping others follow God.

My Bedtime Prayer

God, I want to help others follow you.
Guide me as I take the first step.

As Samuel grew up, the LORD was with him. He made everything Samuel said come true.

1 Samuel 3:19

Night 24

God Speaks to Samuel

Samuel lived at the temple with Eli the priest. One night he heard someone call his name three times. Samuel thought it was Eli, but Eli told him God was calling him. When Samuel heard his name again, he said, "Speak, Lord, I'm listening." Samuel became a wise prophet who delivered God's messages to the people.

Today God's messages are in the Bible. You can listen to God speak to you as you read his words.

My Bedtime Prayer

Lord, speak to me tonight. Help me to listen. I want to know more about you.

"So give me a heart that understands. Then I can rule over your people. I can tell the difference between what is right and what is wrong."

1 Kings 3:9

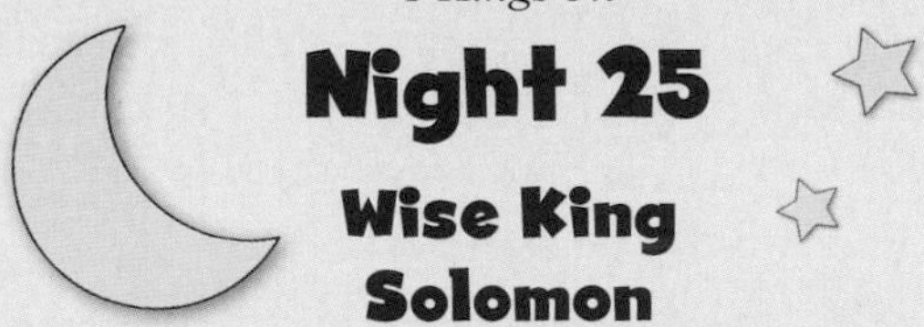

Night 25

Wise King Solomon

One night King Solomon had a dream. God said to him, "Ask for anything, and I will give it to you." King Solomon asked God to give him wisdom so he could understand the difference between right and wrong. God was pleased and gave Solomon a wise and understanding heart. Solomon became the wisest king in the whole world.

If you ask God for wisdom, he will give it to you, and he will be pleased.

My Bedtime Prayer

Give me wisdom, Lord, so I can know what is right and what is wrong.

So Naaman went down to the Jordan River. He dipped himself in it seven times. He did exactly what the man of God had told him to do.

2 Kings 5:14a

Night 26

Naaman Finally Listens

Naaman was an army commander who had a skin disease called leprosy. The prophet Elisha told him to dip in the Jordan River seven times to cure his leprosy. Naaman didn't like this idea. But his servants said, "Just do what Elisha said!" Naaman was wise when he finally listened. He dipped in the river seven times, and his skin disease washed away.

Sometimes God gives us people who can help us. It's wise to listen to them.

My Bedtime Prayer

God, as I go through my day tomorrow, help me truly listen to wise advice from people who love you.

[Josiah] obeyed the Lord with all his heart and all his soul. He obeyed him with all his strength. He did everything the Law of Moses required.

2 Kings 23:25b

Night 27

King Josiah

Josiah was only eight years old when he became the king of Judah. He fixed up the temple so God's people could worship there. A priest found the Book of the Law, and Josiah read it to everyone. Josiah was a wise king because he loved God and wanted to do what was right. Josiah helped the people love and obey God too.

Loving and obeying God is always the right choice.

My Bedtime Prayer

Even though I'm young, Lord, help me love and obey you each day.

"Where is the child who has been born to be king of the Jews? We saw his star when it rose. Now we have come to worship him."

Matthew 2:2

Night 28

The Wise Men

God put a bright star in the sky when Jesus was born. Some wise men saw the star and knew what it meant. They were excited to see Jesus. They followed the star a long, long way until they found Jesus. They gave him special treasures and worshiped him.

Today, we can find Jesus by believing in him. And like the wise men, we can give him our treasures and worship him.

My Bedtime Prayer

Jesus, wise people still look for you.
I want to seek and worship you.

"Mary has chosen what is better. And it will not be taken away from her."

Luke 10:42b

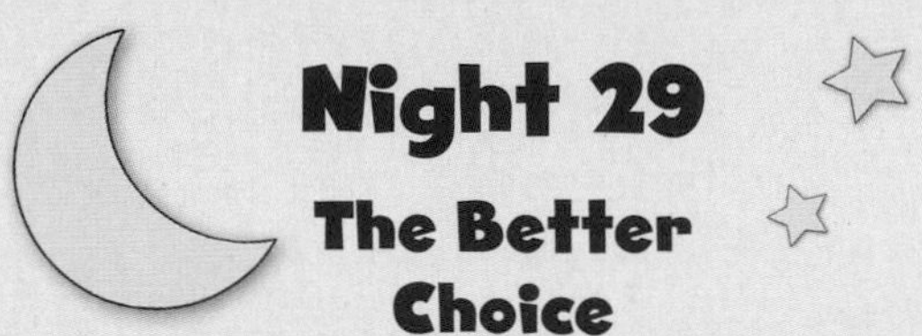

Night 29

The Better Choice

Jesus was at the home of his friends Mary and Martha. Mary sat at Jesus's feet listening to everything he had to say. Martha was upset that Mary wasn't helping her with the work that needed to be done around the house. But Jesus told Martha, "Don't be upset. Mary is listening to me, and that is better."

It's important to work, but we also need to spend time listening to Jesus.

My Bedtime Prayer

Jesus, tonight I'm glad that I can listen to you by reading your words in the Bible.

The crowd was really amazed. They asked, "Aren't all these people who are speaking Galileans? Then why do we each hear them speaking in our own native language?"

Acts 2:7–8

Night 30

Wisdom from the Holy Spirit

After Jesus went to heaven, his followers were meeting together. During one meeting, they heard the sound of wind as small flames appeared on each of them. This was the Holy Spirit God sent to give them wisdom and power to tell others about Jesus. The people who heard them were surprised! They could speak in other languages.

The Holy Spirit is our helper too. You can ask the Holy Spirit to give you wisdom and power to tell others about Jesus.

My Bedtime Prayer

Fill me with your Holy Spirit, Lord.

Praise and Thanksgiving

So Noah came out of the ark. His sons and his wife and his sons' wives were with him. All the animals came out of the ark.

Genesis 8:18–19a

Night 31

Noah Honors God

God kept Noah and his family safe inside the ark while a great flood covered the land. After many weeks and months, Noah's family and all the animals could finally come out. Noah was thankful that God had kept him safe. Noah praised God to honor him. Then God put a rainbow in the sky as a promise to never flood the earth again.

Whenever you see a rainbow, you can thank God for his wonderful promise.

My Bedtime Prayer

Thank you, God, for your rainbow promise. Please keep me safe as I go through my day.

"The LORD gives me strength and protects me. He has saved me. He is my God, I will praise him."

Exodus 15:2

Night 32

Free at Last

God performed a great miracle by helping the Israelites escape from Egypt. After they crossed the Red Sea on dry ground, their hearts were filled with joy because God kept them safe. The Israelites sang a song of praise to thank God for saving them from Pharaoh's army.

God is always good to us. We can thank him with our words or praise him with a song.

My Bedtime Prayer

Thank you, Lord, for the things that brought me joy today.

"The LORD has filled my heart with joy. He has made me strong."
1 Samuel 2:1a

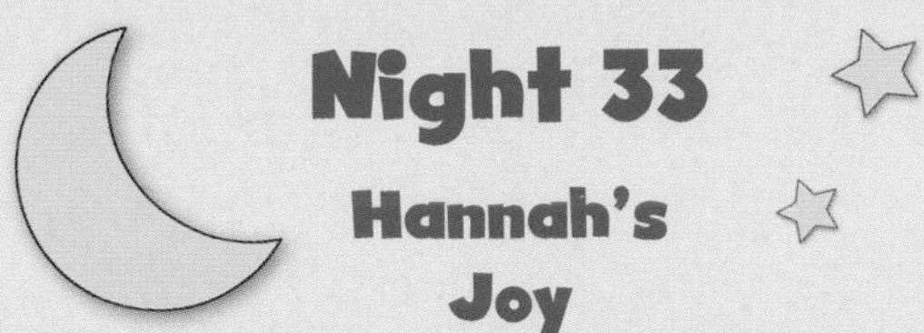

Night 33
Hannah's Joy

Hannah was sad because she didn't have any children. She prayed out loud and asked God to give her a son. "I promise my son will serve you," she said. God heard Hannah's prayer and gave her a son named Samuel. Hannah was so happy she said a prayer of thanksgiving to God.

God listens to our prayers. When he answers them, we can thank him with joy in our hearts

My Bedtime Prayer

Please hear the prayer in my heart tonight, God. Thank you for your love.

"Lord, our Lord, how majestic is your name in the whole earth! You have set your glory in the heavens."

Psalm 8:1

Night 34

Songs of Praise

David liked to play his harp and sing songs to God. He wrote many songs and prayers called psalms. You can read them in the Bible. He often looked into the sky and praised God for his beautiful creation. In many of his psalms, David sings about God's greatness and his love.

Reading the psalms helps us to praise our great God and understand how much he loves us. You can even sing them out loud!

My Bedtime Prayer

Thank you for psalms that help me celebrate your creation and praise you every day, Lord.

"LORD, you are the God of Israel. There is no God like you in heaven above or on earth below. You keep the covenant you made with us. You show us your love."

1 Kings 8:23a

Night 35

A New Place to Worship

King Solomon was thankful that God had chosen him to build the temple for the people of Israel. It took thousands of workers seven years to build the temple with wood, gold, and stone. When the temple was finally finished, the people celebrated their beautiful new place to worship God. The people had worked hard to build a special place to worship God because he is great and deserves our praise.

No one is greater than God, and that is why we praise him.

My Bedtime Prayer

Lord, I will praise and thank you every day because you are a great God.

The shepherds returned. They gave glory and praise to God. Everything they had seen and heard was just as they had been told.

Luke 2:20

Night 36

Happy Shepherds

It was an exciting night when an angel appeared to shepherds who were watching their sheep. The angel said, "Jesus the Savior has been born! You will find him in a manger in Bethlehem." The shepherds ran to the manger. They found baby Jesus and worshiped him. They shared the news with everyone they met and praised God with great joy.

Like the shepherds, we can thank God for Jesus and share the good news with joy.

My Bedtime Prayer

**Thank you, God, for the gift of your Son.
Help me share the good news of Jesus tomorrow.**

When one of them saw that he was healed, he came back. He praised God in a loud voice. He threw himself at Jesus's feet and thanked him.

Luke 17:15–16

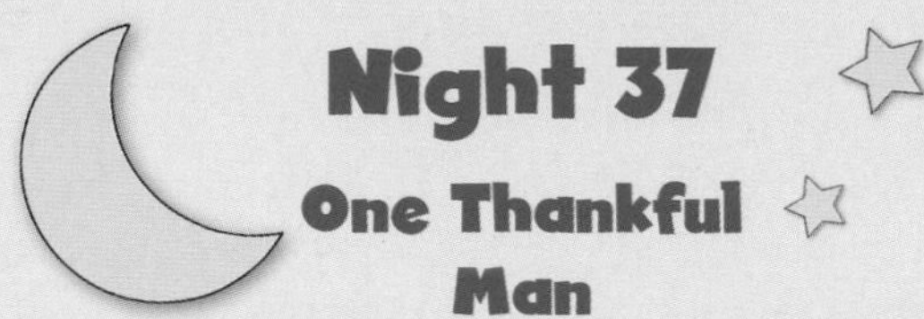

Night 37

One Thankful Man

Ten men with leprosy called out to Jesus as he traveled through their town. "Please heal us, Jesus!" they said. Jesus told them to go and show themselves to the priests. As they walked away, the sores on their skin were all better. They were so happy! But only one man went back to say thank you to Jesus.

When we remember to thank Jesus for what he does, it shows that we have a grateful heart.

My Bedtime Prayer

Lord, please give me a grateful heart for what you've done for me today.

The house was filled with the sweet smell of the perfume.

John 12:3b

Night 38

Mary's Special Gift

Jesus was at the home of his friends, Mary, Martha, and Lazarus. Mary poured expensive perfume on Jesus's feet and wiped his feet with her hair. Judas, who was one of Jesus's disciples, thought this was a waste of money. But Jesus said that Mary was honoring him. Mary's heart was filled with love and thanksgiving for Jesus because he was her Lord and Savior. Jesus deserves our very best gifts of thanksgiving. Nothing is too good for him.

My Bedtime Prayer

Jesus, I want to show how thankful I am for your love.

The whole crowd of disciples began to praise God with joy. In loud voices they praised him for all the miracles they had seen.

Luke 19:37b

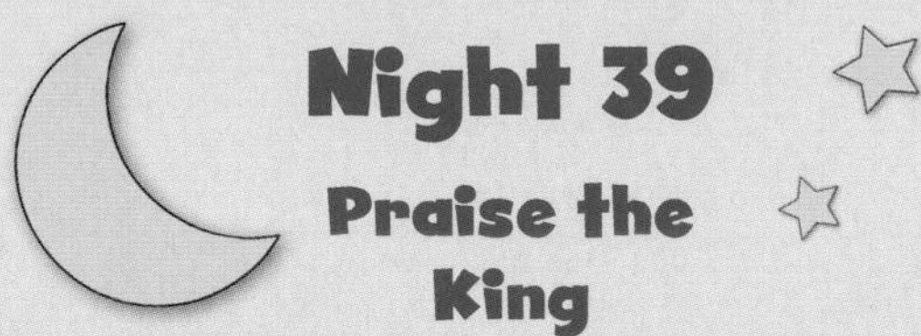

Night 39

Praise the King

During the Passover Feast, Jesus rode a donkey into Jerusalem. His followers cheered and waved palm branches as he rode through town. They were excited and thankful that God had sent him to be their Savior and king. They shouted, "Hosanna! Blessed is the king who comes in the name of the Lord!" Just like Jesus's followers, we can sing praises to thank him for being our Savior and king who rules over everything.

My Bedtime Prayer

Thank you, Lord Jesus. I praise you for being my king every day.

He jumped to his feet and began to walk. He went with Peter and John into the temple courtyards. He walked and jumped and praised God.

Acts 3:8

Night 40

Jumping for Joy

A man who could not walk sat by the temple every day to beg for money. When Peter and John saw him, they said, "We don't have money to give you, but we can do something else for you. In the name of Jesus, stand up and walk!" The man's legs became strong. He jumped up and praised God.

When God uses you to do something great, praise God by giving him the glory. And when God does something great for you, stand up and jump for joy!

My Bedtime Prayer

Tomorrow, fill me with so much joy, God, that I want to jump up and down!

Bullying, Jealousy, and Meanness

*But Isaac said, "Your brother came and tricked me.
He took your blessing."*

Genesis 27:35

Night 41

Jacob Is Jealous

Esau and Jacob were twins. Esau was the older brother and was supposed to get special gifts called a birthright from their father. Jacob was jealous and got Esau to trade his birthright for a bowl of stew. Then Jacob tricked their father, Isaac, into blessing him instead of Esau. Jacob had to run away because Esau was so angry.

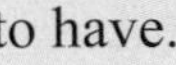

Being jealous can hurt your friends and family. Instead of being jealous, trust God to give you the blessings he wants you to have.

My Bedtime Prayer

God, help me to be happy with what you give me every day.

When Joseph came to his brothers, he was wearing his beautiful robe. They took it away from him. And they threw him into the well.

Genesis 37:23–24

Night 42

Joseph's Mean Brothers

Jacob had twelve sons, and Joseph was his favorite. Jacob made a colorful robe for Joseph, which made his brothers jealous. Then Joseph had some dreams that made his brothers angry. They threw him in a well and sold him to some traders. The brothers were mean to Joseph, but God had plans for him to become an important ruler.

We don't always know why bad things happen, but we can trust that God will be with us no matter what.

My Bedtime Prayer

When I don't understand why things happen, God, help me trust in you.

During the night, Pharaoh sent for Moses and Aaron. He said to them, "Get out of here! You and the Israelites, leave my people! Go. Worship the LORD, just as you have asked."

Exodus 12:31

Night 43

A Stubborn King

Pharaoh was upset that too many Israelites lived in Egypt. He was mean and made them work hard as slaves. God sent Moses to rescue them, but Pharaoh said, "NO WAY!" So God sent plagues, one after another after another, until finally Pharaoh changed his mind. Pharaoh begged the Israelites to leave.

God is greater than any ruler or king or person. He can protect you from people who don't treat you right.

My Bedtime Prayer

God, protect me with your power tomorrow and always.

"If you shave my head, I won't be strong anymore. I'll become as weak as any other man."

Judges 16:17b

Night 44

The Wrong Friends

God gave Samson mighty strength so he could save the Israelites from the mean Philistines. But Samson became friends with a Philistine woman named Delilah. This was not what God wanted him to do. Then Delilah found out the secret to Samson's strength. She cut off his hair while he was sleeping, and God took his strength away.

People who are mean to you are not good friends, even if you want them to be. Ask God to help you have friends who are kind.

My Bedtime Prayer

Help me to have the right kind of friends, God.

Saul tried to pin him to the wall with his spear. But David got away from him just as Saul drove the spear into the wall. That night David escaped.

1 Samuel 19:10

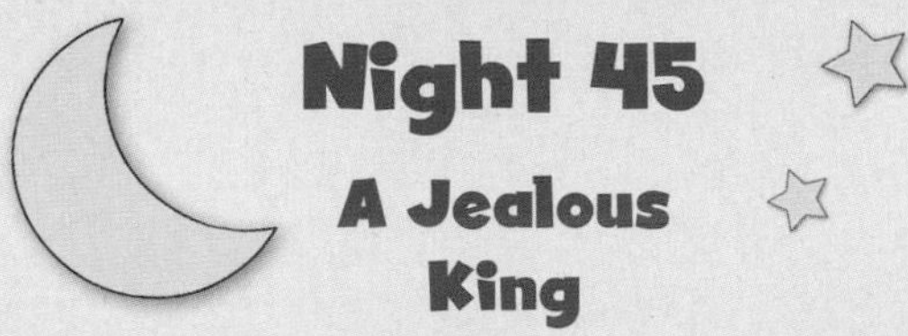

Night 45

A Jealous King

At first King Saul was a good king. He made David the commander of his army. David won many battles, and soon the people liked him better than Saul. This made Saul jealous, and he tried to hurt David. Saul was no longer a good king. He didn't honor God anymore. God chose David to be the next king of Israel.

God is always in control, and he blesses the people who honor him.

My Bedtime Prayer

God, please help me honor and follow you each day.

The king said, "Look! I see four men walking around in the fire. They aren't tied up. And the fire hasn't even harmed them. The fourth man looks like a son of the gods."

Daniel 3:25

Night 46

Nebuchadnezzar's Bad Idea

King Nebuchadnezzar captured some of the Israelites and brought them to Babylon. He made a golden statue and demanded that everyone worship the statue. Shadrach, Meshach, and Abednego loved God. They refused to worship the statue. "Throw them into the fiery furnace!" said the king. The fire did not hurt them because God sent an angel to protect them.

God is the only true God, and no one can make you worship anything or anyone else.

My Bedtime Prayer

God, I will only worship you!

[Herod] said, "Go and search carefully for the child. As soon as you find him, report it to me. Then I can go and worship him too."

Matthew 2:8

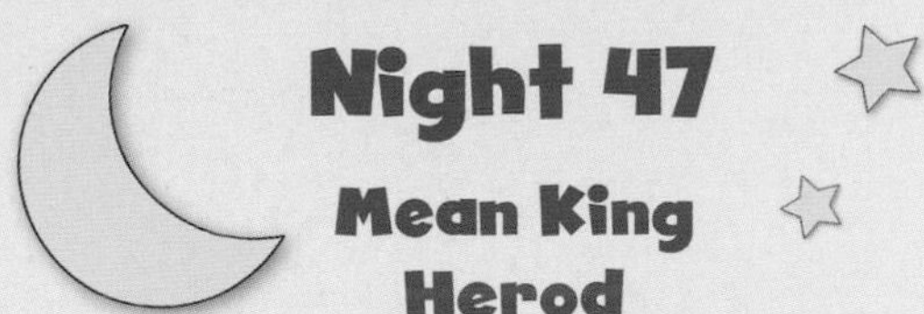

Night 47

Mean King Herod

King Herod was upset when the wise men said a new king had been born. "Tell me where you find him, so I can worship him," he said. But Herod did not want to worship baby Jesus. He wanted to harm him because he did not want anyone else to be king. An angel told the wise men to go home another way so Herod wouldn't see them.

God protected Jesus from a mean and jealous king. Herod's plans did not succeed, but God's plans always do.

My Bedtime Prayer

Your plans are wonderful, God! Thank you for always protecting and guiding me.

There the people who collect the temple tax came to Peter. They asked him, "Doesn't your teacher pay the temple tax?"

Matthew 17:24

Night 48

Bully Tax Collectors

Some tax collectors who were bullies told Peter, "Jesus doesn't pay the temple tax." Jesus told Peter to go fishing. He said, "You will find a coin in the fish's mouth that will be the right amount to pay the tax." Jesus didn't have to pay the tax because he is God's Son, but he did it so they would not be angry.

Ask God to help you know the right thing to do if someone tries to bully you.

My Bedtime Prayer

Lord, help me know how to handle bullies!

While Jesus was still speaking, Judas arrived.
He was one of the 12 disciples. A large crowd was with him.
They were carrying swords and clubs.

Matthew 26:47

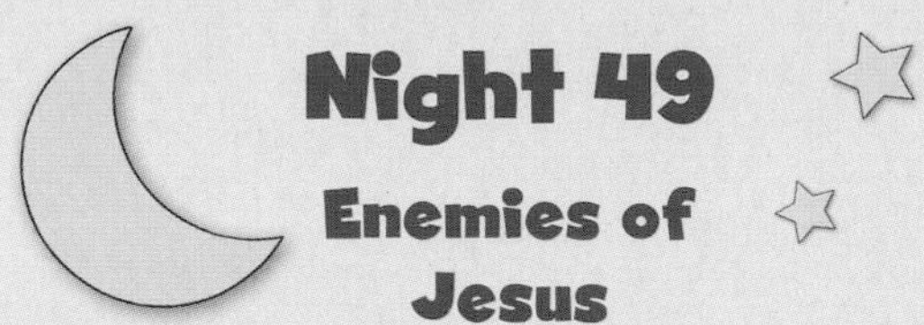

Night 49

Enemies of Jesus

Judas was one of Jesus's disciples, but he turned against Jesus and helped soldiers arrest him. The soldiers mocked Jesus and hung him on a cross because they didn't believe he was God's Son. Jesus was not angry with Judas or the soldiers. He didn't try to hurt them because he knew God had a bigger plan.

When others are mean, we might want to fight back, but that's not what Jesus did. Ask God to help you know what to do.

My Bedtime Prayer

You didn't hurt the people who hurt you, Jesus. Help me to be more like you.

"Who are you, Lord?" Saul asked. "I am Jesus," he replied. "I am the one you are opposing."

Acts 9:5

Night 50

Jesus Changes a Mean Man's Heart

Saul was mean to Jesus's followers. He hurt them and put them in prison. One day a bright light blinded him. He heard a voice say, "Saul, why are you against me?" Saul asked, "Who are you?" The voice said, "I am Jesus." Then Jesus told him how he could see again. Saul's heart changed from hating Jesus to loving Jesus, and his name was changed to Paul.

Jesus can change people's hearts—even if they are mean or cruel at first.

My Bedtime Prayer

Lord, help my heart reflect you.

Forgiving Hearts

So the LORD God drove the man out of the Garden of Eden. He sent the man to farm the ground he had been made from.

Genesis 3:23

Night 51

Adam and Eve Disobey

Adam and Eve enjoyed eating delicious food from the Garden of Eden. But one day they disobeyed God and ate from a tree that God told them not to eat from. They sinned against God and could no longer live in the garden. Even though Adam and Eve sinned, God still loved them, and he forgave them.

God never stops loving us. He forgives our sins when we tell him we are sorry.

My Bedtime Prayer

Forgive me when I sin, Lord.

Esau ran to meet Jacob. He hugged him and threw his arms around his neck. He kissed him, and they cried for joy.

Genesis 33:4

Night 52

Esau Forgives Jacob

Jacob lived with his Uncle Laban, but God told him it was time to go back to his homeland. Jacob was afraid of seeing his brother Esau again. He thought Esau would still be angry because Jacob had been mean to him. But Esau had forgiven Jacob and was happy to see him.

When we forgive others, it takes away the anger that's in our hearts and helps us to be friends again.

My Bedtime Prayer

God, starting tomorrow help me be more forgiving.

Joseph said to his brothers, "Come close to me." So they did. Then he said, "I am your brother Joseph. I'm the one you sold into Egypt."

Genesis 45:4

Night 53

God Meant It for Good

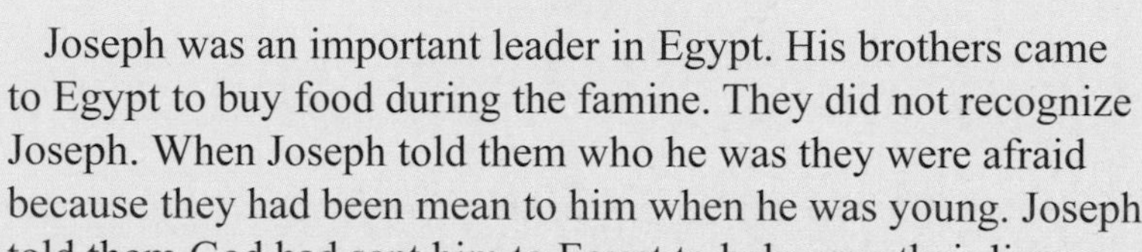

Joseph was an important leader in Egypt. His brothers came to Egypt to buy food during the famine. They did not recognize Joseph. When Joseph told them who he was they were afraid because they had been mean to him when he was young. Joseph told them God had sent him to Egypt to help save their lives.

Joseph forgave his brothers because he trusted God's plan. God is always in control, so even bad things can turn out to be good.

My Bedtime Prayer

God, help me see your plan when things seem all wrong to me.

God saw what they did. He saw that they stopped doing what was evil. So he took pity on them. He didn't destroy them as he had said he would.

Jonah 3:10

Night 54

God Forgives Nineveh's People

God told Jonah to go Nineveh and tell the people to stop doing bad things. Instead of obeying, Jonah got on a ship and ended up in the stormy sea where a big fish swallowed him. Jonah told God he was sorry, so God gave him another chance. The people of Nineveh listened to Jonah's message. They told God they were sorry, and he forgave them.

God is always willing to forgive people who ask him for forgiveness.

My Bedtime Prayer

God, I am sorry for the wrong I did today. Thank you for your forgiveness.

John the Baptist appeared in the desert. He preached that people should be baptized and turn away from their sins. Then God would forgive them.

Mark 1:4

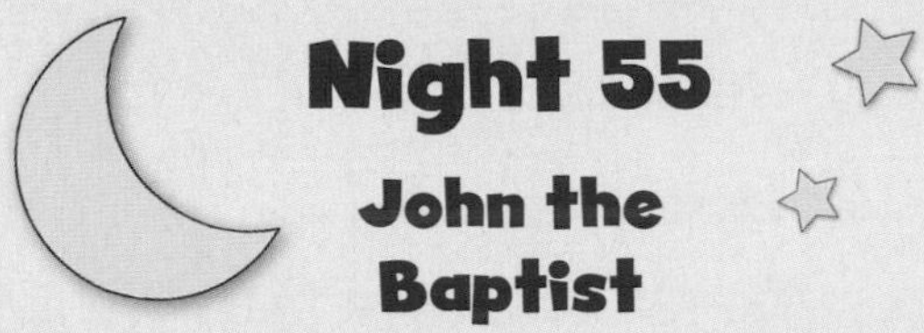

Night 55

John the Baptist

John the Baptist lived in the desert and told people about God. He told them to live in a way that shows their love of God. He told them that Jesus came to save them from their sins. Many people listened to him. They turned from their sins and began to follow God, and John baptized them.

When we believe in Jesus as our Savior, God forgives all of our sins.

My Bedtime Prayer

Jesus, you take away all of my sins. Thank you for being my Savior.

"And forgive us our sins, just as we also have forgiven those who sin against us."

Matthew 6:12

Night 56

The Lord's Prayer

When Jesus was teaching a big crowd, he taught them a prayer called "The Lord's Prayer." The prayer teaches how we can honor God's name when we pray. We can also ask God to give us what we need. Another part of the prayer is about forgiveness. Not only do we ask God to forgive us for the bad things we've done, but we promise to forgive others when they're mean to us.

God will forgive us when we ask him, but he also wants us to forgive others. Forgiving others helps us live the way God wants us to live.

My Bedtime Prayer

Help me to forgive like you do, God.

While the son was still a long way off, his father saw him. He was filled with tender love for his son. He ran to him. He threw his arms around him and kissed him.

Luke 15:20

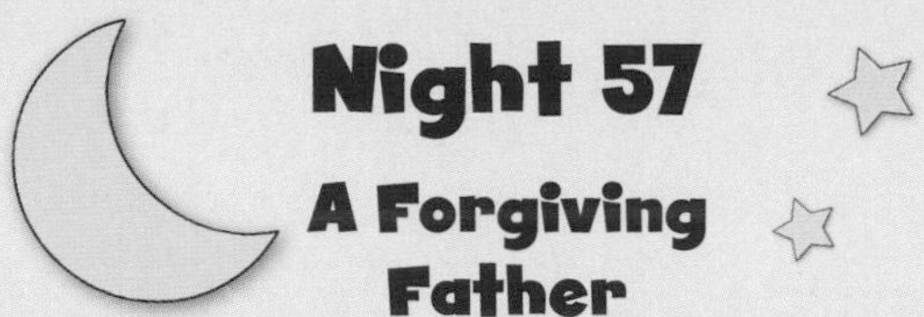

Night 57

A Forgiving Father

Jesus told the story of a man with two sons. The younger son wanted to leave home, so his father gave him some money. The son spent his money on foolish things. Soon his money was gone and he was hungry. He decided to go back home. When the father saw him, he ran to meet him. The father forgave his son and was happy he had come back home.

God is like that father. When we come back to him, God is full of love and happy to forgive.

My Bedtime Prayer

Thank you, God, for loving people who come back to you. Keep me close to you tonight.

Jesus said to Zacchaeus, "Today salvation has come to your house."
Luke 19:9

Night 58

Zacchaeus Meets Jesus

Zacchaeus was a tax collector who took too much money from people. One day he climbed a tree so he could see Jesus better. Jesus said, "I'm coming to your house today, Zacchaeus!" After being with Jesus, Zacchaeus's heart was changed. "I'll give money to the poor and pay back the extra money I took from people," he said. Jesus knew that Zacchaeus was sorry for what he had done.

When we love Jesus, it changes the way we treat people.

My Bedtime Prayer

Jesus, I want to know you better so I can do what is right.

"This is my blood of the covenant. It is poured out to forgive the sins of many people."

Matthew 26:28

Night 59

A Special Supper

Jesus knew he'd be going back to heaven soon, so he had a special supper with his disciples. He took some bread, thanked God, and broke it into pieces. "This is my body," he said. Then he took a cup of wine, gave thanks, and told his disciples to drink it. "This is my blood. It will forgive your sins," he said.

The disciples didn't understand what Jesus's words meant, but soon they would know that forgiveness comes through the blood of Jesus, who died on the cross to be our Savior.

My Bedtime Prayer

**You forgive our sins, Jesus.
Thank you for your great love.**

Jesus said, "Father, forgive them.
They don't know what they are doing."

Luke 23:34

Night 60

Jesus Forgives

Jesus's enemies nailed him to a cross. Jesus's followers were very sad. They couldn't believe this was happening. Jesus loves everyone, even his enemies. He asked God to forgive them for nailing him to a cross. Jesus is God's Son who died to forgive our sins. Whoever believes in him is forgiven.

Jesus is God's Son who came back to life so we can live with him forever.

My Bedtime Prayer

Jesus, thank you for forgiving me today and every day. Give me eternal life.

Serve with Kindness

Abraham looked up and saw three men standing nearby. So he quickly left the entrance to his tent to greet them. He bowed low to the ground.

Genesis 18:2

Night 61

Abraham's Visitors

Abraham saw three men near his tent. He told them to rest under a tree. He didn't know who they were, but he brought them water to wash their feet and gave them something to eat. Abraham took good care of the visitors even before they shared their happy news. "Your wife Sarah is going to have a son," they said.

It's always good to be kind to others. And when we are, sometimes God might surprise us!

My Bedtime Prayer

Help me, Lord, to be kinder tomorrow.

So the men made a promise to her. "If you save our lives, we'll save yours," they said. "Just don't tell anyone what we're doing. Then we'll be kind and faithful to you when the LORD gives us the land."

Joshua 2:14

Night 62

Rahab Protects the Spies

Joshua sent two spies into the city of Jericho. They stayed at a woman named Rahab's house. When soldiers came to capture the spies, she hid the spies on her roof to protect them. The spies promised to be kind to Rahab and protect her because she was kind and protected them.

When people help each other out, it shows their hearts are full of kindness.

My Bedtime Prayer

God, tomorrow I want to be kind by helping others.

"May the Lord reward you for what you have done.
May the Lord, the God of Israel, bless you richly.
You have come to him to find safety under his care."

Ruth 2:12

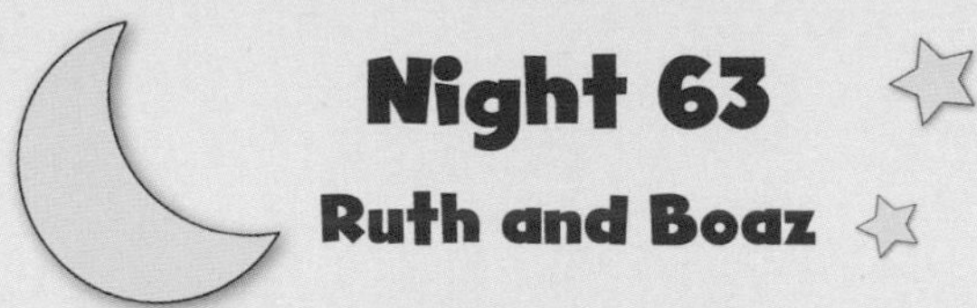

Night 63

Ruth and Boaz

A man named Boaz heard how Ruth had come to Judah to take care of her mother-in-law, Naomi. Boaz showed kindness to Ruth because of the way she cared for Naomi. Boaz let Ruth pick grain from his field and made sure she always had enough. Boaz and Ruth got married, and God blessed them with a baby boy.

When people are kind to others, it shows the goodness that is in their hearts.

My Bedtime Prayer

Lord, fill my heart with kindness and goodness.

She went away and did what Elijah had told her to do. So Elijah had food every day. There was also food for the woman and her family.

1 Kings 17:15

Night 64

Elijah Helps a Poor Widow

Elijah met a poor widow who was gathering sticks. He asked her to make some bread for him. "I only have enough flour and oil for one meal," she said. "Don't worry," said Elijah. "God will take care of you." After the widow made Elijah some bread, her jar of flour was always full, and her jug of oil never ran out.

God takes care of us when we take care of others.

My Bedtime Prayer

Lord, you take care of people who care for others. Help me tomorrow, to show others I care.

Elisha said, "Go around to all your neighbors. Ask them for empty jars. Get as many as you can."

2 Kings 4:3

Night 65

Lots of Jars

A woman said to the prophet Elisha, "I owe a man some money and cannot pay him. All I have is a little olive oil." Elisha told her to get empty jars from her neighbors and pour her oil into the jars. Her neighbors gave her lots of jars. As the woman poured her oil, she filled up every jar! Then Elisha said, "Sell the oil and pay what you owe."

God is pleased when we help others out by sharing.

My Bedtime Prayer

God, help me to share with others tomorrow and every day.

"Let's make a small room for him on the roof. We'll put a bed and a table in it. We'll also put a chair and a lamp in it. Then he can stay there when he comes to visit us."

2 Kings 4:10

Night 66

Elisha's Kind Friends

A woman and her husband lived in the town of Shunem. They invited Elisha to stay with them whenever he was there. They even made a room for him where he could rest. Elisha was thankful for their kindness. The couple didn't have children, so Elisha said, "God will bless you with a baby boy." Elisha wanted God to bless them for being so kind to him.

When others are kind to us, we can ask God to bless them too.

My Bedtime Prayer

Lord, please bless those who were kind to me today.

Jesus said to the servants, "Fill the jars with water."
So they filled them to the top.

John 2:7

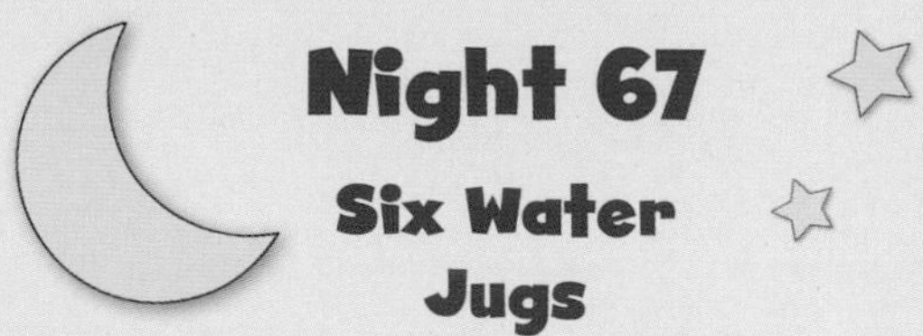

Night 67

Six Water Jugs

While Jesus and his disciples were at a wedding, they ran out of wine. Jesus's mother asked him to help. Jesus told the servants to fill six tall jars with water. When the people tasted the water, it tasted like delicious wine. Jesus did a miracle because he cared about the people at the wedding and didn't want things to go wrong.

Jesus cares about everyone. He treats us all with love and kindness.

My Bedtime Prayer

Thank you for caring about me, Jesus.
I felt your love today.

"Here is a boy with five small loaves of barley bread. He also has two small fish. But how far will that go in such a large crowd?"

John 6:9

Night 68

A Boy Shares His Lunch

A big crowd had come to see Jesus. It was getting late, and the people were hungry. A kind boy gave Jesus two fish and five small loaves of bread. "That won't be enough to feed 5,000 people," said the disciples. But it was more than enough! Jesus blessed the food, and his disciples passed it around to everyone. The boy generously gave what he had to Jesus, and Jesus used it to bless him and others.

When we offer our gifts to Jesus, he can do amazing things with them.

My Bedtime Prayer

**Tomorrow, with your help,
I can do great things, Jesus!**

*"The man they call Jesus made some mud and put it on my eyes.
He told me to go to Siloam and wash. So I went and washed.
Then I could see."*

John 9:11

Night 69

Jesus Heals a Blind Man

Jesus and his disciples walked by a man who was blind. Jesus said the man was blind so that God could do a miracle in his life. Jesus put mud on his eyes and told him to wash it off. The man did what Jesus said, and then he could see.

Jesus's miracles showed that God had sent him, and that God loves his people. Jesus loves people too and wants to help them.

My Bedtime Prayer

Thank you, Jesus, for the way you show your love and kindness.

[Jesus] poured water into a large bowl. Then he began to wash his disciples' feet. He dried them with the towel that was wrapped around him.

John 13:5

Night 70

Jesus Serves His Disciples

Jesus and his disciples were sharing a special meal. The disciples were surprised when Jesus filled a bowl with water and began washing their feet. That was something a servant usually did. Jesus wanted to show his disciples that if they really loved God, they needed to serve other people.

Jesus gave us an example of what it means to serve others. He wants us to show love and kindness to them.

My Bedtime Prayer

Help me to serve others all week long, Jesus.

Peace, Hope, and Patience

"I am with you. I will watch over you everywhere you go. And I will bring you back to this land. I will not leave you until I have done what I have promised you."

Genesis 28:15

Night 71

Jacob Has a Dream

Jacob traveled far away to his uncle Laban's house. One night while he was going, Jacob dreamed about some angels going up and down a stairway to heaven. God spoke to Jacob and said, "I am with you, Jacob, and will watch over you. I will give your family all of this land." When Jacob woke up, he felt happy and peaceful. He knew God would always watch over him.

When you want to feel peaceful, remember that God is watching over you right now.

My Bedtime Prayer

I'm happy you are always with me, God.

The Israelites ate manna for 40 years. They ate it until they came to a land where people were living. They ate it until they reached the border of Canaan.

Exodus 16:35

Night 72

God Feeds the Israelites

The Israelites were hungry when they lived in the desert, but God did not forget about them. He sent quail in the evening and manna in the morning. When they were thirsty, God gave them fresh water from rocks. The Israelites needed to be patient and trust God to give them what they needed.

Like the Israelites, we can be patient and trust God to give us what we need. God does not forget about us.

My Bedtime Prayer

God, you gave me what I needed today! Thank you.

Then a message came to Elijah from the Lord. He said, "Leave this place. Go east and hide in the Kerith Valley ... You will drink water from the brook. I have directed some ravens to supply you with food there."

1 Kings 17:2–4

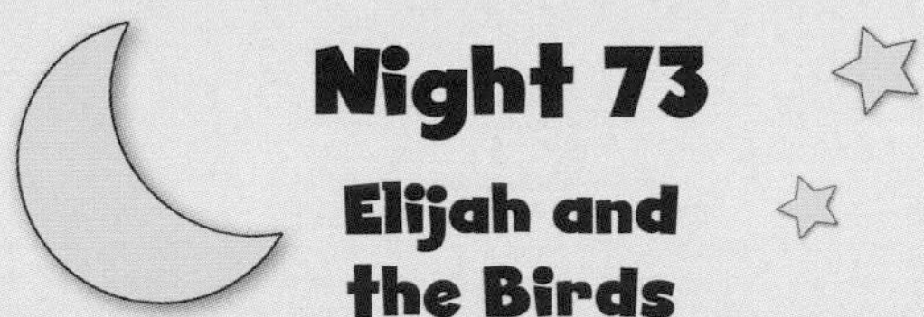

Night 73

Elijah and the Birds

Elijah told King Ahab it would not rain for a long time, and that made the king angry. God told Elijah to go away and hide. Elijah went where God told him to go. He drank water from a brook, and God sent birds to bring him food. Elijah was not afraid of King Ahab.

Elijah had peace knowing that God would take care of him. God takes care of people who love and trust him.

My Bedtime Prayer

God, thank you for taking care of me today.

The angel greeted her and said, "The Lord has blessed you in a special way. He is with you."

Luke 1:28

Night 74

Mary's Special Message

The angel Gabriel had a special message for Mary. "You will give birth to God's son. His name will be Jesus." Mary didn't understand how this could be because she wasn't married. "Don't be afraid," said Gabriel. "All things are possible with God." Mary loved God. Her heart was full of hope and peace as she waited for God's perfect plan.

If we love God, we can trust his plan for our lives and be filled with peace.

My Bedtime Prayer

Lord, trusting you gives me hope and peace as I lay down to sleep.

While Joseph and Mary were there, the time came for the child to be born.

Luke 2:6

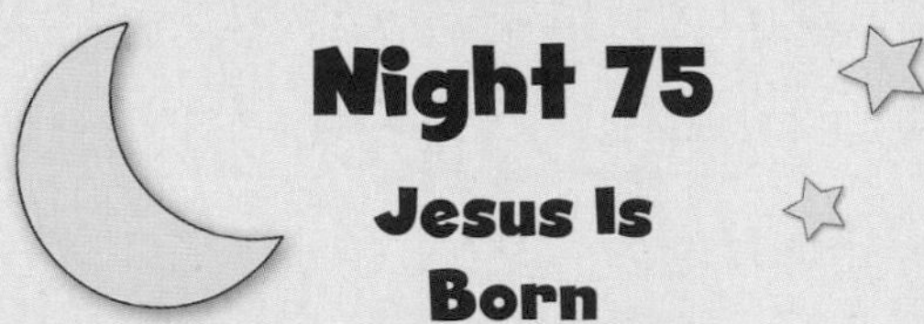

Night 75

Jesus Is Born

From the very beginning, God promised that he would send his Son to earth to save people from sin. After thousands of years, Jesus was born in the town of Bethlehem. Jesus would make things right between people and God.

By believing in Jesus, we have the hope of living with him in heaven forever and ever. Even in dark times, Jesus brings hope to the whole world!

My Bedtime Prayer

Jesus, thank you for the hope you bring the world every day.

*"May glory be given to God in the highest heaven!
And may peace be given to those he is pleased with on earth!"*

Luke 2:14

Night 76

Peace on Earth

On the night Jesus was born, an angel announced the good news to shepherds who were watching their sheep. Then a choir of angels began praising God, "Glory to God on high! Peace on earth and goodwill to all."

Jesus came to bring peace to a world filled with troubles. When we believe in Jesus, we can have peace in our hearts no matter what is happening around us.

My Bedtime Prayer

**Jesus, knowing you love me
fills me with peace tonight.**

"Lord, you are the King over all. Now let me, your servant, go in peace. That is what you promised."

Luke 2:29

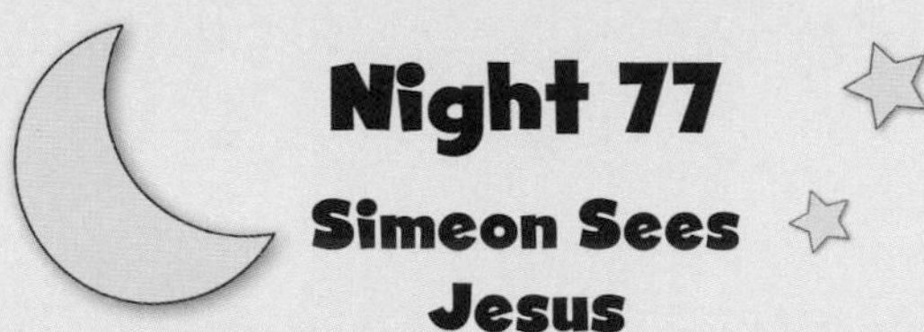

Night 77

Simeon Sees Jesus

Simeon believed in God's promise to send a Savior to the world. The Holy Spirit told Simeon he would live to see the Savior, so he patiently waited for many years. When Simeon met Joseph, Mary, and baby Jesus at the temple, he knew Jesus was the Savior. He held Jesus in his arms and praised God.

It's hard to be patient when we are looking forward to something. But everything happens in God's time, and his timing is always right.

My Bedtime Prayer

God, help me to be patient and wait for things to happen in your time.

The commander replied, "Lord, I am not good enough to have you come into my house. But just say the word, and my servant will be healed.

Matthew 8:8

Night 78

A Commander's Faith

The commander of an army had a servant who was very sick. He knew Jesus could heal him. The commander placed his hope and faith in Jesus. He told Jesus to speak the words and his servant would be healed. Jesus was pleased with the commander's faith. He healed his servant just by speaking the words.

Jesus is pleased when our faith is strong, and when we trust him to bring us happier days.

My Bedtime Prayer

Jesus, tomorrow I will put my faith and hope in you.

The disciples were amazed. They asked, "What kind of man is this? Even the winds and the waves obey him!"

Matthew 8:27

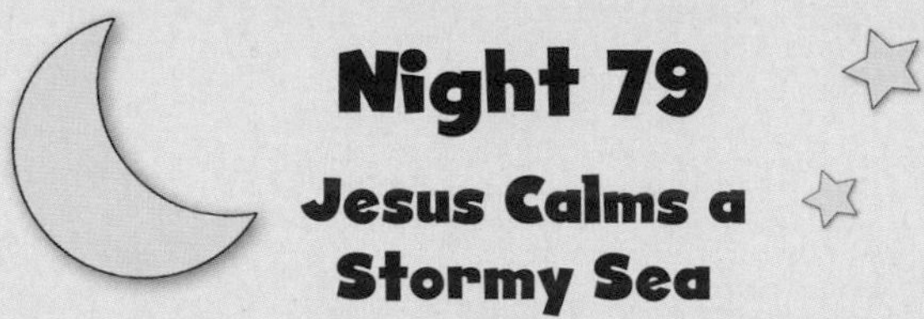

Night 79

Jesus Calms a Stormy Sea

Jesus and his disciples were in a boat when a big storm came up. The disciples were afraid as the wind and waves rocked their boat. They woke up Jesus and cried, "Save us! We're going to drown!" Jesus told the storm to stop, and suddenly the lake was calm and peaceful.

Anytime you are afraid or nervous, you can call out to Jesus. If he can bring peace to a stormy sea, he can bring peace to your heart.

My Bedtime Prayer

Lord, when I am afraid you give me peace.

*"Look! I am coming soon! I bring my rewards with me.
I will reward each person for what they have done."*

Revelation 22:12

Night 80

Jesus Is Coming Back

After Jesus went to heaven, his disciple John had a vision. Jesus told John about the happy and beautiful things in heaven and how there would be a new heaven and earth someday. He said, "I am coming back to make everything right."

When Jesus returns, he will rule over heaven and earth. When we look at the world's many troubles, it can be hard to wait patiently for Jesus, but his promise to return gives us hope.

My Bedtime Prayer

Jesus, I will wait for you to come back and make things new.

Loving God and Loving Others

Noah was a godly man. He was without blame among the people of his time. He walked faithfully with God.

Genesis 6:9

Night 81

Noah Loved God

When God created the world, everything was good. But after a while, people turned away from God and broke his heart. God decided to send a flood to wash everything away. But God saw that Noah loved him. He told Noah to build an ark for his family and lots of animals. Noah loved God so much that he did exactly what God told him to do.

God kept Noah safe and promised he would not send another flood like that again. God is pleased when people love and follow him.

My Bedtime Prayer

God, tomorrow, help me love you like Noah did.

"I am the LORD your God. I brought you out of Egypt. That is the land where you were slaves. Do not put any other gods in place of me."

Exodus 20:2–3

Night 82

The Ten Commandments

When the Israelites were living in the wilderness, God gave Moses the Ten Commandments to teach the people how he wanted them to live. The first four commandments are about loving God. The remaining six commandments are about how to treat other people.

The commandments God gave the Israelites are for us too. God wants us to love him more than anything else and show love and kindness to others.

My Bedtime Prayer

God, help me obey your commandments this week.

Then the LORD said, "Get up and anoint him. This is the one."
1 Samuel 16:12b

Night 83

David's Heart for God

God wanted a new king for Israel, so he sent Samuel to a man named Jesse. Samuel looked at Jesse's sons and thought the biggest and strongest one should be the king. But God chose David, the youngest son, because David loved God with his whole heart. God doesn't look at the outside of a person. He sees what's in their heart.

It doesn't matter how big or strong we are. What matters is how much we love God. He chooses people who love him.

My Bedtime Prayer

Give me a heart that loves you, Lord.

I am sure that your goodness and love will
follow me all the days of my life.
And I will live in the house of the LORD forever.

Psalm 23:6

Night 84

David's Sheep

When David was growing up, he spent many years taking care of his father's sheep. He watched over the sheep and protected them from wild animals. He led them to places where they could nibble on green grass and drink fresh water from streams.

In Psalm 23 David says God loves his people just like a shepherd loves his sheep. When we understand how much God loves us, it's easy for us to love God back!

My Bedtime Prayer

God, protect and guide me tomorrow.
I can feel your love.

[Elijah] prayed, "LORD, you are the God of Abraham, Isaac and Israel. Today let everyone know that you are God in Israel.

Let them know I'm your servant."

1 Kings 18:36b

Night 85

The One True God

Elijah worshiped God, but King Ahab worshiped a false god named Baal. Elijah and the king met on Mount Carmel where they each built an altar. "Ask your god to send fire to the altar," said Elijah. Ahab prayed and prayed, but nothing happened. Then Elijah prayed to the one true God. Fire came down from heaven and burned up everything!

Elijah proved that he loved and worshiped the one true God, and we can love and worship him too.

My Bedtime Prayer

God, you are the only God I love and worship.

[Anna] gave thanks to God. And she spoke about the child to all who were looking forward to the time when Jerusalem would be set free.

Luke 2:38

Night 86

Anna at the Temple

Anna loved God very much. She was a prophet who lived at the temple. Anna prayed to God every day and night. One day, Mary and Joseph brought baby Jesus to the temple. Anna saw him and thanked God for sending his Son. Anna was so happy, she told everyone at the temple about Jesus, the Savior of the world.

Everyone who loves God can tell others about Jesus. Then the whole world will know.

My Bedtime Prayer

This week, Lord, help me tell others about Jesus.

He answered, "'Love the Lord your God with all your heart and with all your soul. Love him with all your strength and with all your mind.' And, 'Love your neighbor as you love yourself.'"

Luke 10:27

Night 87

The Good Neighbor

"Who is my neighbor?" asked a teacher of the law. Jesus answered with a story. "A man was beaten by robbers who stole everything from him. A priest walked by but didn't help him. A temple worker didn't help him either. When a Samaritan saw him, he bandaged the man's wounds and brought him to an inn to rest. Now who was the good neighbor?" The teacher replied, "The Samaritan."

Jesus wants us to care about others the way the Samaritan did. When we see someone in need, we should help them and show them God's love.

My Bedtime Prayer

God, help me look for ways to be like the Samaritan tomorrow.

"What I'm about to tell you is true," Jesus said.
"That poor widow has put in more than all the others."

Luke 21:3

Night 88

The Widow's Coins

One day Jesus was at the temple when people came to put their money in the collection box. Some rich people put in a lot of money. Then a poor widow who loved God put two small coins into the box. Jesus saw her offering. Even though the others put in more money, Jesus said she gave the most because she gave everything she had.

What we give to God shows how much we love him.

My Bedtime Prayer

Lord, I promise to give you my best tomorrow.

When Jesus and the disciples had finished eating, Jesus spoke to Simon Peter. He asked, "Simon, son of John, do you love me more than these others do?" "Yes, Lord," he answered. "You know that I love you."

John 21:15

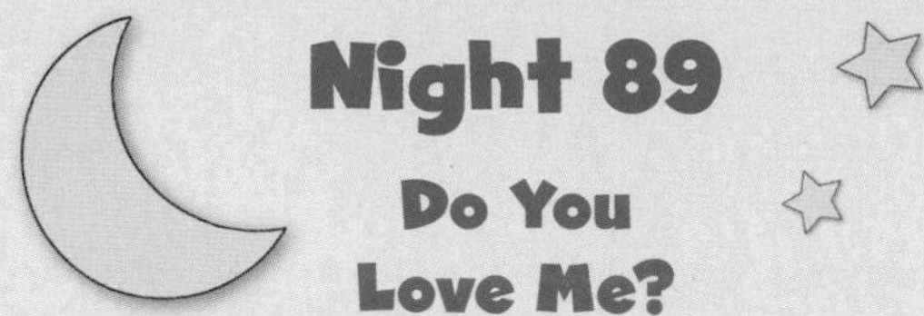

Night 89

Do You Love Me?

The disciples fished all night but didn't catch anything. Jesus called from the shore, "Throw your nets to the other side of the boat." Soon their net was full of fish. Peter jumped in the water and swam to Jesus. "Do you love me?" Jesus asked. "You know I love you," said Peter. "Then feed my sheep," Jesus said.

Jesus's sheep are the people who follow him. If we love Jesus, then we will love and care for his people.

My Bedtime Prayer

**Jesus, I want you to know I love you.
Help me show love to others too.**

"We are telling you the good news. What God promised our people long ago he has done for us, their children. He has raised up Jesus."

Acts 13:32–33

Night 90

Paul Shares the Good News

After Paul became a follower of Jesus, he traveled to many places telling everyone he met about him. Paul loved Jesus and wanted other people to love him too. Paul baptized people and started churches. Many people became followers of Jesus because Paul explained to them that God sent Jesus to save us from our sins.

God wants us to love Jesus so much that we share the good news with everyone.

My Bedtime Prayer

Jesus, help me to share your good news.

God's Purpose for Us

Then God said, "Let us make human beings so that they are like us. Let them rule over the fish in the seas and the birds in the sky. Let them rule over the livestock and all the wild animals. And let them rule over all the creatures that move along the ground."

Genesis 1:26

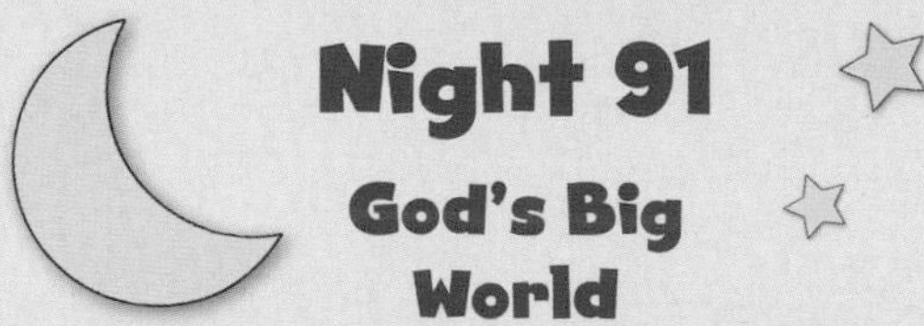

Night 91

God's Big World

In the beginning, God created our beautiful world. He made the sun, moon, and stars. He made the land and sea. God made fish and birds and every animal that crawls, runs, or climbs. God liked what he made, but he wanted someone to enjoy his wonderful creation. So God made a man and woman who were the first people to live on earth.

God wants us to enjoy his world and care for everything he made.

My Bedtime Prayer

Thank you, God, for creating our wonderful world. Help me take good care of it every day.

There the Lord *mixed up the language of the whole world. That's why the city was called Babel. From there the* Lord *scattered them over the whole earth.*

Genesis 11:9

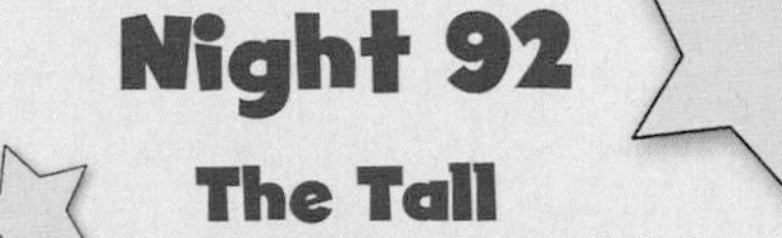

Night 92

The Tall Tower

After the Great Flood, everyone spoke the same language. The people decided to work together to build a tower all the way to the sky, so everyone would know how great they were. They acted as if they didn't need God anymore. So God mixed up their language so they could not work together on the tower.

It's okay to have big plans and dreams, but it's not okay to forget about God. No matter what we plan or dream, we always need God.

My Bedtime Prayer

God, show me your will in all that I do this week.

When the child grew older, she took him to Pharaoh's daughter.
And he became her son. She named him Moses.
She said, "I pulled him out of the water."

Exodus 2:10

Night 93

God's Plans for Baby Moses

An Israelite woman had a baby boy. The baby boy was in danger, so she put him in a basket and placed it in the river. Pharaoh's daughter found him. The princess let Moses's mom take care of him while he was a baby. Moses grew up in the palace because God had plans for him. Someday he would lead all the Israelites out of Egypt.

God has a plan for everyone's life. As you grow up, you can pray and ask God to show you his plan.

My Bedtime Prayer

God, help me know your plan for my life.

The Israelites continued their travels. Whenever the cloud lifted from above the holy tent, they started out. But if the cloud didn't lift, they did not start out.

Exodus 40:36–37

Night 94

A Cloud over the Tent

When the Israelites lived in the desert, God told them to build a tent called a tabernacle. God placed a cloud over the tent. When the cloud stayed over the tent, the people stayed where they were. When the cloud moved, the people would follow it. The Israelites always knew where God wanted them to go.

Today, we can ask God to lead us where he wants us to go, and then we can follow him.

My Bedtime Prayer

Tomorrow, lead me where you want me to go, God.

John is the one Isaiah the prophet had spoken about.
He had said, "A messenger is calling out in the desert,
'Prepare the way for the Lord. Make straight paths for him.'"

Matthew 3:3

Night 95

God's Purpose for John

God had a special purpose for John the Baptist's life. John taught people about God's forgiveness and told them how God wants us to live. He baptized many people in the river. "Someone greater than I is coming to save you," he said. John was talking about Jesus. And one day, Jesus asked John to baptize him.

No matter what purpose God has for us, we can tell people about Jesus.

My Bedtime Prayer

Thank you, God, that you have a special purpose for my life.

"Again, the kingdom of heaven is like a net. It was let down into the lake. It caught all kinds of fish."

Matthew 13:47

Night 96

The Good Fish

Jesus told a story to a big crowd. He said, "Some fisherman caught a lot of fish in their net and brought them to shore. They kept the good fish and tossed out the bad ones." Jesus said this to help them understand that the good fish are people who belong to God's kingdom.

God wants us to join his kingdom, and we can do that by believing in Jesus.

My Bedtime Prayer

Thank you, God, that I belong to your kingdom through Jesus.

*"Then he will call his friends and neighbors together.
He will say, 'Be joyful with me. I have found my lost sheep.'"*

Luke 15:6

Night 97

The Lost Sheep

Jesus taught that God is like a shepherd and his people are like sheep. He said, "If one sheep wanders away, the shepherd will search until he finds it. Then he has a big celebration." That's how God feels about his people.

When we wander away from him, it makes God sad. But when we come back to God and tell him how much we love him, he celebrates with the angels in heaven.

My Bedtime Prayer

Lord, help me to not wander far from you in the days ahead.

People were bringing little children to Jesus.
They wanted him to place his hands on them to bless them.
Mark 10:13

Night 98

Jesus and the Children

When grown-ups were bringing their children to Jesus, the disciples told them to go away because they thought Jesus was too busy. But Jesus said, "Let the children come to me! My kingdom belongs to them." Jesus took the children in his arms. He put his hands on them and blessed them.

You don't have to wait until you grow up to have a place and purpose in his kingdom. Jesus loves all his children, and that means you!

My Bedtime Prayer

Be with me and bless me as I go to sleep, Jesus.

So you must go and make disciples of all nations. Baptize them in the name of the Father and of the Son and of the Holy Spirit.

Matthew 28:19

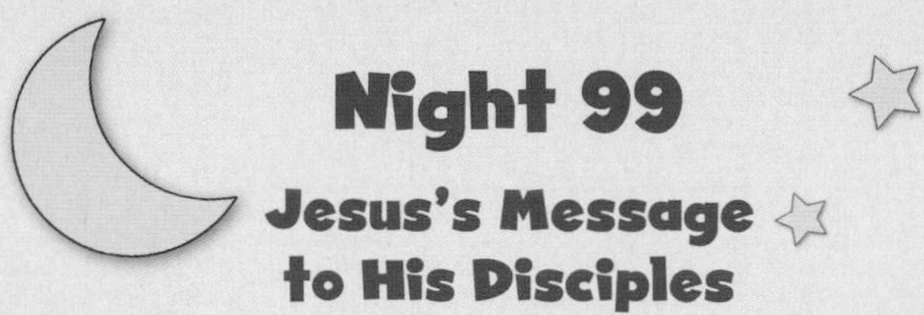

Night 99

Jesus's Message to His Disciples

After Jesus came back to life, he told his disciples that he would soon be going to heaven. Then he gave them a very important assignment. Jesus said, "Go all over the world and tell other people about me. Make new disciples and teach them to obey my commandments."

Someday God may have a special assignment for you too. Until then, keep reading the Bible to learn more about his plans for you.

My Bedtime Prayer

Thank you, Jesus, that I can learn more about you every day.

The believers studied what the apostles taught. They shared their lives together. They ate and prayed together.

Acts 2:42

Night 100

New Believers Meet Together

As the disciples taught people about Jesus, many people believed in him. The new believers wanted to learn more about God, so they met together in people's homes to study and pray. They shared everything they had. That is how the first churches started.

God's purpose for us is to meet other people, help each other, and pray together. We can keep doing this until the day that Jesus returns.

My Bedtime Prayer

Thank you that I can be with other people who love you, Jesus.

Building foundations of faith with children for over 30 years!

9780310750130
Hardcover

The Beginner's Bible® has been a favorite with young children and their parents since its release in 1989 with over 28 million products sold. While several updates have been made since its early days, *The Beginner's Bible*® will continue to build a foundation of faith in little ones for many more years to come.

Full of faith and fun, *The Beginner's Bible*® is a wonderful gift for any child. The easy-to-read text and bright, full-color illustrations on every page make it a perfect way to introduce young children to the stories and characters of the Bible. With new vibrant three-dimensional art and compelling text, more than 90 Bible stories come to life. Kids ages 6 and under will enjoy the fun illustrations of Noah helping the elephant onto the ark, Jonah praying inside the fish, and more, as they discover *The Beginner's Bible*® just like millions of children before. *The Beginner's Bible*® was named the 2006 Retailers Choice Award winner in Children's Nonfiction.

More products from *The Beginner's Bible*® to discover:

The Beginner's Bible
Little Lamb's Christmas
9780310770589

The Beginner's Bible
First 100 Bible Words
9780310766858

The Beginner's Bible
Learn Your Letters
9780310770244

The Beginner's Bible
All Aboard Noah's Ark
9780310768678

The Beginner's Bible
Super Girls of the Bible
Sticker and Activity Book
9780310751182

The Beginner's Bible
Preschool Workbook
9780310751670

The Beginner's Bible
I Can Read
Jonah and the Giant Fish
9780310743286

The Beginner's Bible
People of the Bible
9780310765035